YARD SALE

Written by Danielle Carl

Illustrated by Sally Jo Vitsky

Harcourt Achieve

Rigby • Saxon • Steck-Vaughn

www.HarcourtAchieve.com
1.800.531.5015

This is the Price family.
Their home is too full.
They are having a yard sale.

The Prices make a sign.

They make price tags.

They can't wait for the yard sale to begin!

People come to the yard sale.
Everyone likes the things for sale.
Everyone wants to buy something.

Mrs. Grace wants to buy a lamp.
"But it's my favorite lamp," Mrs. Price explains.
"I'm sorry, the lamp is not for sale."

Eddie wants to buy a piggy bank.

"But it was my first piggy bank," Pete Price explains.

"I'm sorry, the piggy bank is not for sale."

Celia wants to buy a picture.

"But a friend gave it to me," Mr. Price explains.

"I'm sorry, the picture is not for sale."

7

The Parks want to buy a clock.

"But we love to hear it ring," the Prices explain.

"We're sorry, the yard sale is over."

The Prices put everything back inside.
Their home is still very full.
It's just the way they like it!

Close
AND
Turn

Your ten dollars is gone. How did you spend it?
You bought things you needed and wanted.
It's fun to go shopping!

muffin $1

hat $5

book $2

ball $2

Close AND Turn

You want a new toy to play with.
You can buy a ball for two dollars.
Which ball do you want?

You are hungry for something to eat.
You can buy a muffin for one dollar.
Which muffin do you want?

You need a book for school.
You can buy a book for two dollars.
Which book do you want?

It's cold outside. You don't have a hat.
You can buy a hat for five dollars.
Which hat do you want?

Let's go shopping!

You have ten dollars to spend.

What do you need? What do you want?

Let's $hopping!

Written by Danielle Carl

Harcourt Achieve

Rigby • Saxon • Steck-Vaughn

www.HarcourtAchieve.com
1.800.531.5015